D1243846

Groundwood Books / House of Anansi Press
110 Spadina Avenue, Suite 801
Toronto, Ontario M5V 2K4
or c/o Publishers Group West
1700 Fourth Street, Berkeley, CA 94710

We acknowledge for their financial support of our
publishing program the Government of Canada through
the Canada Book Fund (CBF).

Library and Archives Canada Cataloguing in Publication
Wolfsgruber, Linda
A daisy is a daisy is a daisy (except when it's a girl's name)
/ Linda Wolfsgruber.
Translation of: Daisy ist ein Gänseblümchen.
ISBN 978-1-55498-099-4
1. Feminine names — Juvenile literature. 2. Names, Per-
sonal — Juvenile literature. 3. Flowers — Nomenclature
(Popular) — Juvenile literature. 4. Flowers — Juvenile
literature. I. Title.
CS2369.W6413 2011   j929.4'4   C2010-905909-3

The illustrations consist of drawings, collage and
monotype, with some sewing machine stitching and
tempera.

Design and lettering by Michael Solomon
Printed and bound in China

A daisy is a daisy is a daisy (except when it's a girl's name)

by Linda Wolfsgruber

GROUNDWOOD BOOKS / HOUSE OF ANANSI PRESS Toronto Berkeley

Fleur ~ French

Floraigh ~ Gaelic

Florka ~ Hungarian

Flora ~ Latin girl's name

Lore ~ Basque girl's name

Florica ~ Romanian girl's name

Kukka ~ Finnish girl's name

Zvetana ~ Bulgarian girl's name

Hana ~ Japanese girl's name

Flora, Florica, Kukka, Lore, Hana and Zvetana mean flower.
Flowers are born in the spring.

Katina ~ Slavic

Blathnat ~ Irish

Perah ~ Hebrew

Turkish girl's name

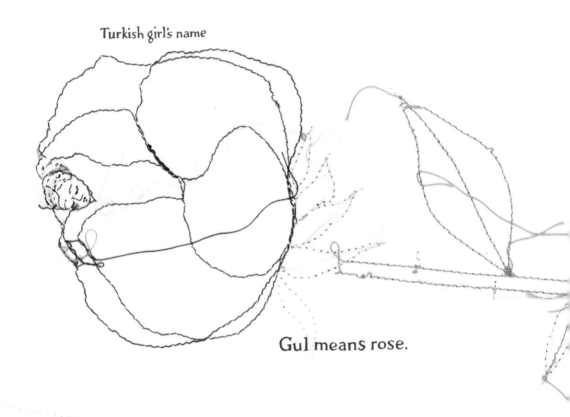

Gul means rose.

Rosa ~ Spanish   Rhodanthe ~ Greek   Raisa ~ Hebrew   Briar ~ English

Erika means heather.

German girl's name

Hadley~English
(heather meadow)

Hebrew girl's name

Nurit means buttercup.

Portuguese girl's name

Girassol means sunflower.

Chamania ~ Hebrew
Clytie ~ Greek

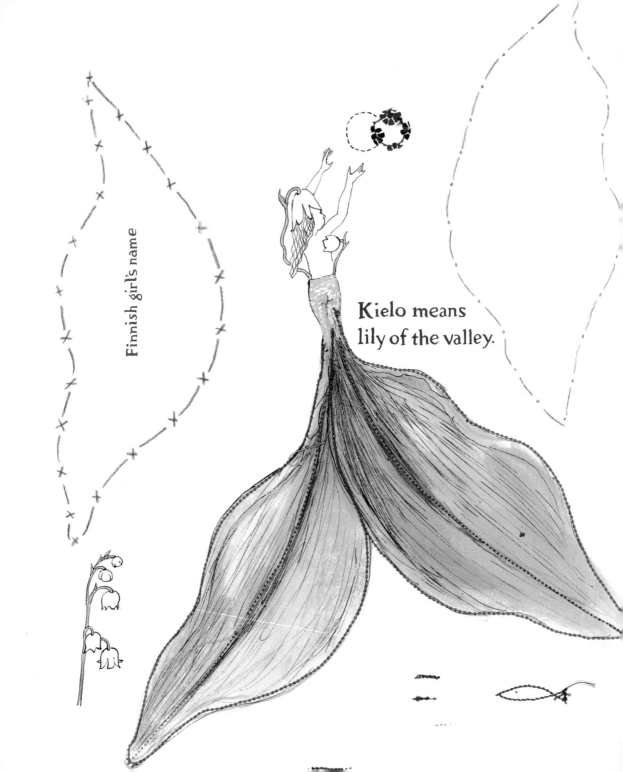

Finnish girl's name

Kielo means
lily of the valley.

Spanish girl's name

Margarita   means daisy.

Marguerite ~ French
Shasta ~ Native American
Daisy ~ English

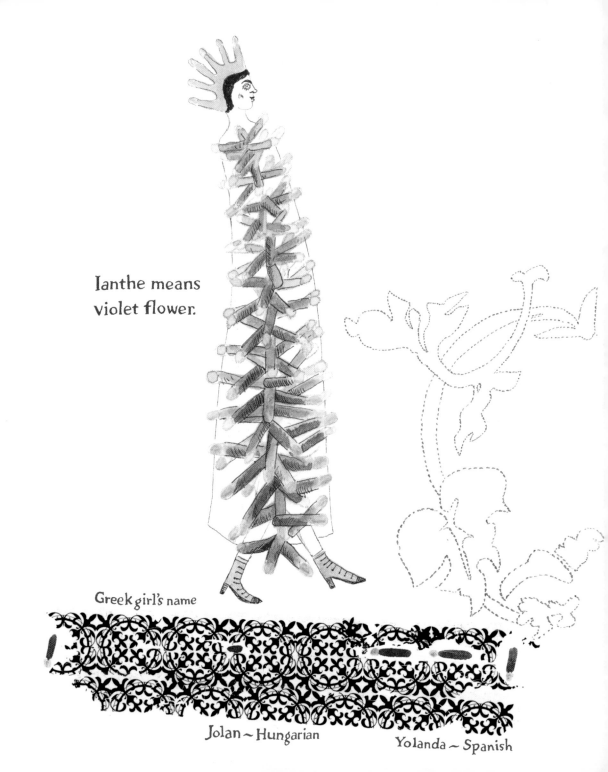

Ianthe means
violet flower.

Greek girl's name

Jolan ~ Hungarian

Yolanda ~ Spanish

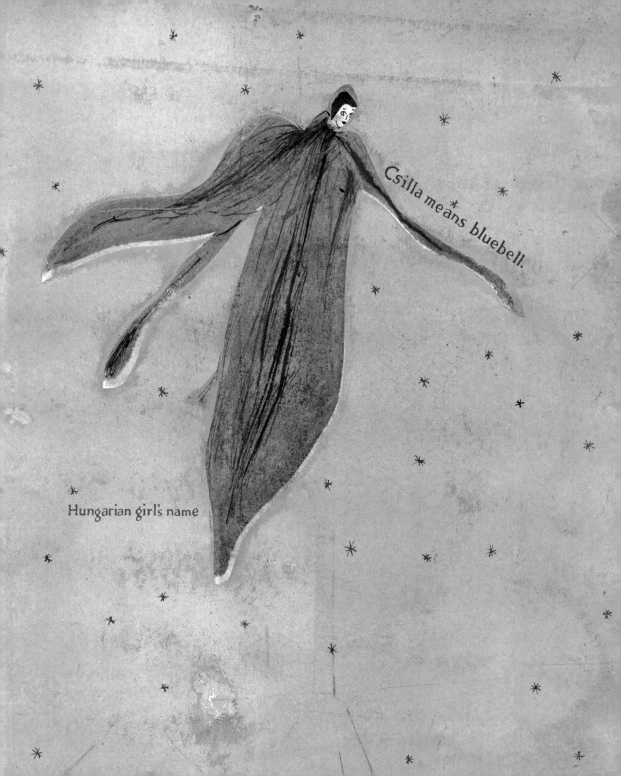

Csilla means bluebell.

Hungarian girl's name

Berfin means snowdrop.

Kurdish girl's name

Eirlys ~ Welsh

Swedish girl's name

Linnea means small mountain flower.

Jacinda means hyacinth.

Spanish girl's name

Jakinda ~ Basque

Giacinta ~ Italian

Zahra Sahara means desert flower.   Arabic girl's name

Dutch girl's name

Mirte means myrtle.

Hadassah ~ Hebrew

Mirta ~ Spanish and Greek

Kamilka means camomile flower.

Slavic girl's name

Sakura means cherry blossom. Japanese girl's name

Yasmina ~ Arabic

Jasmine ~ French

Jasmin ~ English

Persian girl's name

Jasaman means jasmine.

Yasiman ~ Hindi

Gelsomina ~ Italian

Violette means violet.

French girl's name

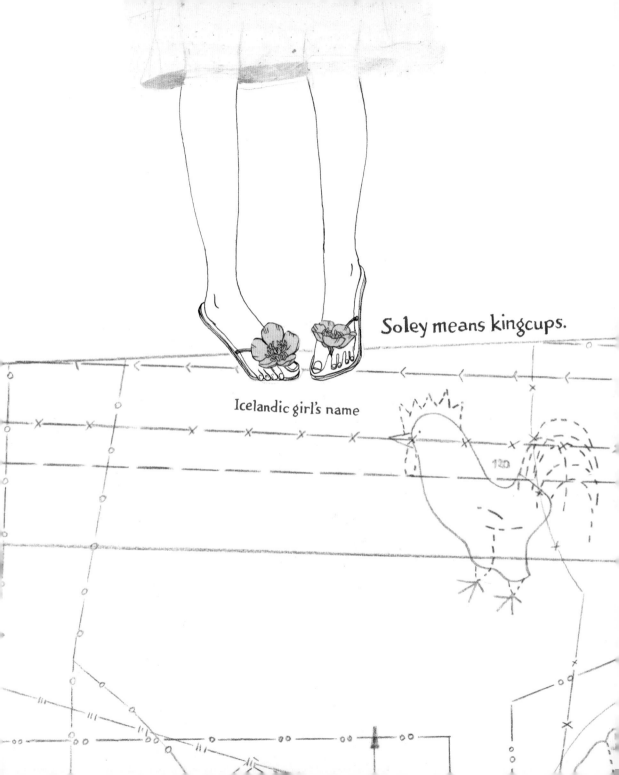

Soley means kingcups.

Icelandic girl's name

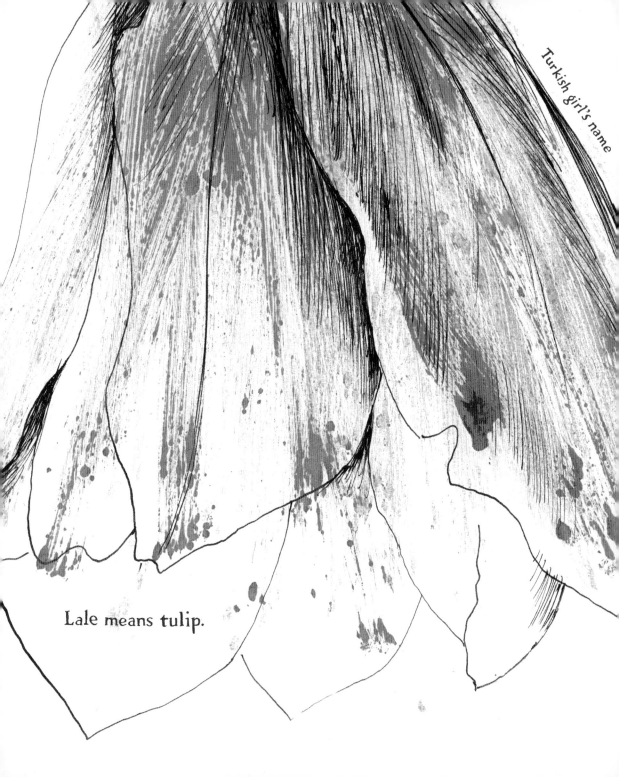

Turkish girl's name

Lale means tulip.

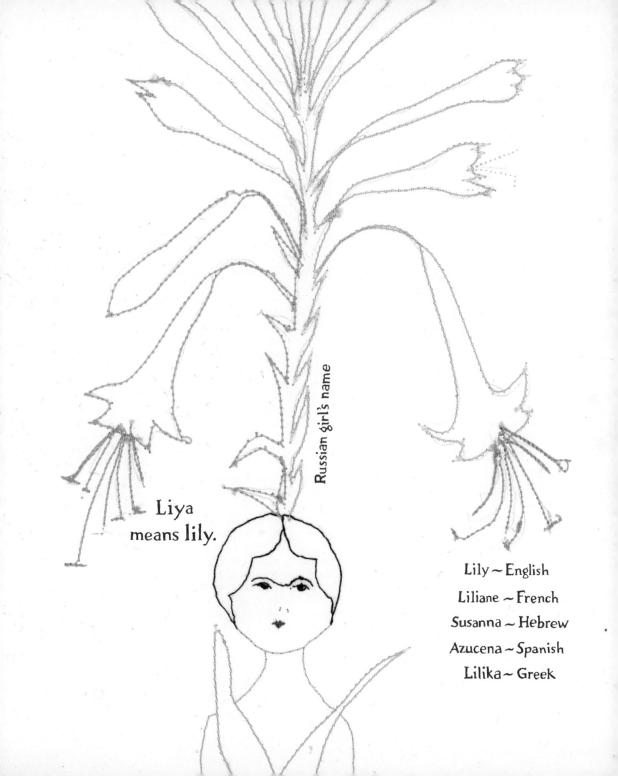

Russian girl's name

Liya
means lily.

Lily ~ English
Liliane ~ French
Susanna ~ Hebrew
Azucena ~ Spanish
Lilika ~ Greek

Poppy means poppy.

English girl's name

Pola ~ Arabic

Amapola ~ Spanish

Greek girl's name

And Chloe is a very young sprout...

who is sleeping quietly under the snow,